Divinity In Divorce
Power In Gratitude & Love

"Whether you are growing together or growing apart
this book will save you a heart ache."
~ Dr. John F. Demartini, Bestselling author of *The Heart of Love*

Divinity In Divorce
Power In Gratitude & Love

Dr. Dena G. Churchill

INTERNATIONAL HEALTH PUBLISHING
February 22, 2008
A Publishing Group Exposing the Truth

Published by:
International Health Publishing
Carrollton, TX USA
www.InternationalHealthPublishing.com
phone: (978) 846-1964
e-mail: writer@InternationalHealthPublishing.com

All rights reserved, including the right of reproduction in whole or in part in any form or by any means, electronic or mechanical, including photocopy, recording, or any information storage and retrieval system, without written permission from the publisher and author; except by a reviewer who may quote brief passages in review.

The author is not offering medical advice or recommending any treatment, technique, or therapy without the direct or indirect consultation of a physician. The content within this book is intended as information of a general nature. The publisher and the author assume no responsibility for your actions.

Copyright © 2010 by Dena G. Churchill
First paperback printing January 2010

Divinity In Divorce – Power In Gratitude & Love
By Dr. Dena G. Churchill

ISBN-13   978-0-9818353-4-1
ISBN-10   0-9818353-4-1

Library of Congress Control Number: 2009943445

SAN   856-6925

10 9 8 7 6 5 4 3 2 1

Dedication

There are many to thank and acknowledge throughout my divorce and book preparation, but none of this would be possible without my former spouse (*FS*). He is the one to whom I dedicate this book and offer my sincere love and gratitude for this journey.

Foreword

Divorce is just a word. The circumstances surrounding divorce you create for yourself. Divorce is a courageous journey with a tremendous opportunity for growth, filled with inspirational ideas and divine moments waiting to be experienced. Written by a divorced woman, this book is fundamentally intended for both spouses, and by extension children or other family and friends, to help them each thrive through the divorce. Generalizations are made based on my heterosexual spousal relationship with children, however some of the names, details, characters or situations may be enhanced or neglected to present this manuscript to the masses with divine guidance and without prejudice.

These pages hold the paths of possibilities for you. Perhaps my journey and resources may at the very best offer you a new empowered perspective, and at the very least, let you know that you are not alone. Let this divorce be the testing ground for the next divine lesson. In the words of our *Star Wars* gurus approaching any courageous endeavor: "May the force be with you."

Contents

1. Divinity And The Wax Maker — 1
2. Thank God For My Divorce — 5
3. Legal Lingo — 19
4. Swim In Stress — 25
5. The Kids Will Be Okay — 33
6. Laugh It Out — 41

Divorce Quotes — 42
Appendix A – Performance Breath — 47
Appendix B – Affirmations To Abundance — 51
References — 55
About Dr. Dena G. Churchill — 57
What Others Are Saying — 59

1

Divinity And The Wax Maker

Divinity is such a cosmic word to pair with a commodity such a divorce. Who on earth puts these two terms together? I shall, as it holds the essence to the answer that I sought of how to find a path of love and gratitude through my divorce.

The concept of *divinity* retains a personal definition, depending on the clan from which you come and the authority to whom you give power. So allow me to suggest a few synonymous terms that may reflect your own philosophies and religiosities: *divine power, universal intelligence, innate wisdom, Grand Organized Design* (*GOD* according to Dr. John Demartini), *Holographic Universe* (Michael Talbot), and *Divine Matrix* (Greg Braden). Simply, that which is often outside of our perception and gives order to our world by being omnipotent (all being), omnipresent (all present) and omniscience (all knowing). If we assume that our world is based on our own perception, then a position where all perceptions are seen at once is a greater awareness of intelligence. This greater awareness of intelligence is my divinity.

The human mind consciously exists in a duality of input and output; a divine awareness relies on a panoramic view of one's surroundings based on trust, belief, experience, and ultimately acceptance and confidence in all possibilities. Many authors define intelligence as the duality of input – receiving a stimulus from the environment – and output – actively responding to that stimulus. In addition to this linear pattern of learning, the human mind has the ability of thought, reason, logic, as well as the ability of deducing a certain outcome in a quantum realm.

Rene Descartes maintains that the mind is the foundation of knowledge, outside the limitations of human senses. Descartes is a 17th Century French philosopher who popularized the phrase: "I think therefore I am." In his wax demonstration, he notes that a piece of wax when brought to a flame changes its characteristics from a solid to a liquid. Even though the human senses input data as a change in form, the mind must deduce and trust that both forms are indeed wax. Therefore, in order to properly grasp the nature of the wax, one cannot use the senses. One must use the mind. Descartes concludes, "And so something which I thought I was seeing with my eyes is in fact grasped solely by the faculty of judgment which is in my mind."

As humans, we have the ability to choose our thoughts and perspective. The mastermind exercises included in this book help to create a map for navigating out of the prison of fears and doubts in the mind, and into the freedom and energy in a heart of love. Can we hold our perception and at the same time realize that the exact opposite perception also exists? Within the concepts of this book you will witness love transforming as if wax melting into different forms of marriage and divorce. I invite you to step outside the box of your senses and find the alternate perspectives that exist along your journey.

The experience of being able to see these different forms, and understanding that they are all parts of a loving matrix surrounding us every minute of our lives, grants us the faith, trust, confidence and security in a force at work outside of ourselves. The key to divinity is within the ability to expand perceptions to a higher level of understanding.

Divinity in Divorce: Tranquility In Gratitude & Love

2
Thank God For My Divorce

One's first thought would probably not be to thank God for struggles and challenges. However, in the midst of a storm it is important to remain safe, as well as protected. Feeling victimized, traumatized by divorce, or even burdened by tormenting thoughts of how the divorce may impact your life can be overwhelming. Once you gain the courage to even say the word *divorce,* you may cry. The journey begins into the scary unknown with surging fears and emotions. The first step towards moving into acceptance is always the hardest: admitting divorce first to yourself, and then telling someone else. Once the idea and intention has been established, your divorce *celebration* begins. I purposefully use the word *celebration* to illustrate that the process is how you choose to perceive it. While you may fall into a million little pieces, it is a period of massive growth with an opportunity to learn to love yourself and others.

Let me see if I can list some of your thoughts and questions. I know them well because they were once mine, too. *How can I do this financially? What about the kids? Where will I live? What will people think? Maybe things will change? How can I handle this turmoil? What about my spouse; I do not wish to hurt him/her? He/she is just thinking about him/her-self. Does he/she not see he/she is the cause of this? How could he/she lie to me? This will drive us both crazy? I do not know what he/she will do? At this stage in my life, will I ever find another? What are the legalities? Who will be there to support me? Am I making a mistake?*

Divorce is a death and a rebirth all in one package; so much so, I compare these initial stages of emotion in divorce to Kubler Ross's *Stages Of Grief In Death*:

- **D**enial (this is not happening to *me!*)
- **A**nger (why is this happening to *me?*)
- **B**argaining (I promise I'll be a better person *if...*)
- **D**epression (I don't *care* anymore)
- **A**cceptance (*I'm ready* for whatever comes)

The final stage that I add to the Kubler Ross construct of denial, anger, bargaining, depression, and acceptance, is *gratitude*. This stage hosts the shell-breaking enthusiasm allowing for rebirth.

Your spouse will be asking himself the same questions you are asking yourself, and the world according to him will look just a grim and fearful. There is your perception and then there is his perception – both laced with the poisons of emotions such as fear, anger, grief, and resentment. If you step outside yourself, floating to the corner of the room, both perspectives may be viewed and a more clear reality will present.

Dr. John Demartini has developed a tool called the *Demartini Method*^{TM} instrumental in creating a place of greater awareness. Now I must admit, it took several seminars before I could let go of my victim mentality and my ego to truly allowed myself to experience this process in its entirety. However, once accomplished the miracle of liberation was priceless for the four lives it affected: my spouse, our two children, and mine.

At the onset of my pending separation, I called this behavioral expert with the question of how to get through a divorce with love and gratitude, thinking there would be a magical phrase, recommendation or solution. However, it took me years to discover the answers I sought were within me all along. I just had to get out of my own way to see them.

The following brief illustration does not perform justice to the *Demartini Method*. You will be reading it on an intellectual level rather than the emotional and spiritual plane I experienced first-hand. The experiential wisdom and understanding for your unique situation only arrive through answering the questions for yourself with the hours of exercise in your own workbook. You dictate your destiny. People wishing to fully empower themselves will participate in the full course, finding their own answers and feeling their own heart open to the power of love.

To begin moving through the *Demartini Method* towards understanding, I was asked to list the qualities I *liked* and the qualities I *disliked* about my former spouse (*FS*). The list of *dislikes* could have gone on forever. But the list of what I liked was very short. In fact, I was so emotionally charged and resentful initially, I could only think of two traits I liked about him. My short loving list of traits included that he loaded the dishwasher in a space-conserving manner and that he shined his shoes well. With a lot of sweat and tears, I eventually pulled out a few more to fill up the page.

Then, as part of my process, I was to identify all of the traits I disliked in him in myself. This exercise in reflection was most difficult. I am not *like him*. I am the exact opposite of him (which evidently I have discovered is why the universe pulled us together in the first place, and I will discuss this later in this chapter). I am not an angry person; I am not aggressive; the *"I am not's"* continued, as I resisted to see myself as a reflection of him.

But as Dr. John Demartini says, "We all have every trait. This is a law." Some may be stingy with their money and some may be stingy with their sexual intimacy, but we are all stingy in some capacity.

In retrospect, I did occasionally become angry; and as a chiropractor, many days required me to be aggressive with my adjustments. I have been verbally abusive with a telemarketer, and with the publicist that tried to tell me how I should write my press release. Further, I did lie occasionally to the dental hygienist about how often I floss, and to my children about a white-bearded Christmas character; I did lie about how many lovers I had, and to the telemarketing survey consultant. The sobering result was seeing a clear reflection that I possessed to the same degree every quality I criticized him for possessing. In some shape, I too characterized them all, even if in a slightly different form. The traits I was denying most in myself were the ones to which I was most criticizing of him.

The next part of this process was realizing other people would describe my *FS* in an exact opposite way than I had listed. His family and friends, our neighbors, and his co-workers and staff would describe him differently. Uniformly, there would be people equal in magnitude describing me differently than he might, depending upon who is looking through the scope. Through this exercise I came to realize my descriptors were just *my* labels, my own perspective. Naturally, those that share my values would agree with me, while those that share his would agree with him.

The third component was in understanding how the 'labeled' negative traits were beneficial, and also how positive traits may actually have been a dis-service. I know what you may be thinking, *How can yelling at someone be beneficial? How does lying serve anyone?* This too was so difficult for me to see, I almost walked-out of the two-day seminar I had paid for in advance. My strong desire to release my own anger, coupled with not wanting to loose my monetary investment and the fear of Dr. John Demartini embarrassing me, kept me glued to my seat. Among the swear words floating through my thoughts as I struggled to find *benefit* in 'negative' traits, I continued harvesting my mind for an answer.

After a few months I found one. Support sustains us, but at last, challenge helps us grow. Dr. Demartini poses the question, *"Which is more loving, support or challenge?"*

The final part of the process was realizing there is an equal and opposite force present synchronously in time and space, what Dr. Demartini calls the *God Principle* (*Grand Organized Design*) – an intelligence in the universe keeping all in a balance. For example, the same moment your *FS* is criticizing you someone is praising you. Alternatively, the moment someone criticizes you, your *FS* or someone else comes to your rescue.

Discovering the blessings in perceived adversity invites love and grace into your heart, and promotes liberation from the emotional turmoil in your mind. A challenge may have brought you closer to another family member or friend, or even given you an opportunity to prioritize your values and desires, bringing you closer to your purpose. As one relationship is dissolving, another is simultaneously reappearing. Maybe you will need to see four new relationships emerge in order to balance the magnitude of one marriage that is dissolving, but it will present. Don't be afraid to look.

The last nail to crack the cage around my heart was the realization that *if* my former spouse acted in the exact opposite way, I would not have liked this any better. This level of realization – when finally fulfilled – is an acceptance that all is perfect just as it *is*. In other words, only through the challenge of him being him, am I me.

I gained strength and certainty of my values and purpose, found new relationships to provide new lessons, and by believing in myself, discovered an inner resourcefulness. For, in the midst of the minefield I found my own diamond. Acceptance is revealed in the phrase *"I forgive you,"* but also hosts an imbalanced perspective, as it assumes your way is still more right and their way needs forgiveness. The work is complete with empowerment in life and its divine experience when you attain a level of gratitude, saying and feeling the *"Thank you. I love you. I would not change you."* These phrases reflect the understanding in the blessing of what *is*. Beyond the verse of *"I forgive you,"* I grew into singing the chorus of true love, rejoicing: *"Thank you for this style of love and learning!"*

Dr. John Demartini is a visionary in creating this Nobel Prize-worthy methodology for unearthing divinity. I thank him for his mentorship and contributions to humanity. Historically though, I must mention, there have been many others to assist with defining similar principles, as we are all borrowing ideas from the same reservoir of universal wisdom.

With humble grace, I present the following quotes and passages from this reservoir of wisdom to exemplify love in its many forms, and the perfection existing within each moment.

"If we could understand the order of the universe well enough, we would find that it surpasses all the wishes of the wisest and that it is impossible to make it better than it is."
~ G.W. Leibniz

Excerpt from Kahlil Gibran's *The Prophet*, *(p. 5-7)*

Speak to us of Love.
And he raised his head and looked upon the people and there fell a stillness upon them. And with a great voice he said:
When love beckons to you, follow him,
Though his ways are hard and steep.
And when his wings enfold you yield to him,
Though the sword hidden among his pinions may wound you.
And when he speaks to you believe him,
Though his voice may shatter your dreams as the north wind lays waste the garden.

For even as love crowns you so shall he crucify you. Even as he is for your growth so is he for your pruning.
Even as he ascends to your height and caresses your tenderest branches that quiver in the sun,
So shall he descend to your roots and shake them in their clinging to the earth.
Like sheaves of corn he gathers you unto himself.
He threshes you to make you naked.
He sifts you to free you from your husks.
He grinds you to whiteness.

He kneads you until you are pliant;
And then he assigns you to his sacred fire, that you may become sacred bread for God's sacred feast.
All these things shall love do unto you that you may know the secrets of your heart, and in that knowledge become a fragment of Life's heart.
But if in your fear you would seek only love's peace and love's pleasure,
Then it is better for you that you cover your nakedness and pass out of love's threshing–floor,
Into the seasonless world where you shall laugh, but not all of your laughter and weep, but not all your tears.

Love gives naught but itself and takes naught but from itself.
Love possesses not nor would be possessed, For love is sufficient unto love.
When you love you should not say, "God is in my heart", but rather "I am in the heart of God."
And think not you can direct the course of love, for love if it finds you worthy, directs your course.

Love has no other desire but to fulfill itself.
But if you love and must needs have desires, let these be your desires:

To melt and be like a running brook that sings its melody to the night.
To know the pain of too much tenderness.
To be wounded by your own understanding of love;
And to bleed willingly and joyfully.
To wake at dawn with a winged heart and give thanks for another day of loving;
To rest at the noon hour and meditate love's ecstasy;
To return home at eventide with gratitude;
And then to sleep with a prayer for the beloved in your heart and a song of praise upon your lips.

The universe apparently thrusts complimentary opposites together and calls them the *full quantum of love*. So, in an attempt to have us love more of ourselves and our world, we are given a mirror. As we move through our lessons of love, there is more clarity reflected with the recognition of the profound truth that we are all *one* in spirit. That which we cannot love, we will attract until we do. So the ultimate goal is to love all the parts of yourself; including the greed, the ego, the liar, the cheater, the aggressor, as well as others characteristics you may already love to own, such as compassion, caring, and kindness. People you meet (particularly spouses – who love you the most) will appear different to you, opposite in fact. Opposites do attract. If two people were both the same, one would be redundant. Differences draw you together for the purpose of love and learning.

By now you may be seeing the contradiction that I went through in my minds' journey. The question arose, *"If everything is perfect just as it is, then why even divorce?"* For a period of time, I went through a mental oscillation, as we all do when our string has been plucked. And to complicate matters, as I changed my mind, my husband would move in the opposite direction (a physics principle I came to know later as *'spooky action at a distance'*). First I wanted the divorce, then he, then I. My mind felt like a plate of assorted biscuits.

First I had to see how leaving the marriage would serve me, but as I was empowering myself I worried for him. Once I could see the benefits of empowerment and opportunity for both of us in our divorce, the oscillations stopped. I gained the confidence to move on. I realized the challenge of the divorce would empower our family to greater heights of strength, confidence and love. I found love and gratitude when I realized I am who I am because he is who he is, but my ego began wanting the next challenge. So, I guess you could say I had to truly love him and myself before I could leave the marriage.

To further clarify, do you ever really leave or lose anything? The Law Of Thermodynamics, outside an atomic phenomenon, says that energy is conserved through space and time, so there are no losses or gains, just transformations. Dr. Demartini says, *"The masses live in this world of gains and losses, the masters live in a world of transformation."*

The marriage relationship transforms into a divorce relationship, into a former spouse relationship. You will always remain a family unit, but the form will appear differently; meaning, there will be a transformation of the family into a new definition and unique identity. New supports and challenges in the same or different form will present. For example, if the challenges from your former spouse disappear, then challenge will reappear in another form, such as being witness to a friends' divorce, a family illness, a financial crisis, etc. The bitter, the sweet and the sour are ever present allowing us to tastes all the flavors of life. In sharing my deepest personal insights through my process, I hope it may inspire you to taste them all.

Before the *Demartini Method*, I was questioning God. I asked questions such as, *"How could He put me in such a situation? What do I have to learn?"* Full of fear, anger and resentment, I felt ready to leave my husband.

Since the *Demartini Method*, I understand that the traits I considered most challenging were incredibly my greatest teachers. Addicted to the peace and pleasure of love, the healing and construction of the body, I attracted a combat system engineer to teach me the balance.

As I am learning to love all parts of myself – mean and nice, cruel and kind, warful and peaceful – I see my *FS* as one of my greatest teachers of all parts of love, in or out-of our marriage. His challenge and questioning of my purpose was a test of my commitment. Even the shared custody arrangement – despite initially tearing my heart in two – was a gift to our boys, giving them a dedicated father with presence. The free time while the children are away opens the door for me to follow the second part of my purpose in writing and speaking to the hearts and souls of others.

There are daily challenges and emotions rising and falling with the tides, but I now have the tools to talk myself away from the ledge, to find love and wisdom within each. I thank God for my divorce.

3

Legal Lingo

Divorce, in many instances means to "divide by force." The emotions of grief and anger during the dissolution of a marriage are often embedded into a dance of dividing the assets. Matrimonial law in itself is quite clear, the assets and liabilities are divided equally. Divorce lawyers are necessary when this law is challenged from one side or the other. My recommendation to those considering divorce is to read this book before proceeding. Pretend the dissolution is a business deal – void of all emotion – and agree to separate without force. You may then refer to your separation as a "divide" instead of a "divorce." This way, you conserve energy, time, and money. Otherwise, your inability to compromise can feed a divorce lawyer a delicious income at a rate ranging somewhere between $500-$900 per hour.

The length of a marriage and the addition of children during the marriage paint more color onto your binder. But once again, there are laws governing marital divorce situations based on salaries and assets before the marriage even began. Generally, the nurturers like to hold on to the kids and the home, while the providers to their savings and pensions. But through the separation, you both will greatly transform your portfolios, learning new ways of growing and of being resourceful. Let go a little and trust in the process. Ask yourself, "Would it injure my children to spend more time with my partner? Did my partner's contribution to the family assist me in saving and making money? If I had not been married with the resources and benefits the marriage brought, how would my situation look currently?" Further ask how has the person you are divorcing contributed to your life? Are you thinking outside the box of emotion in your decisions? If not, ask a neutral friend or a friend of your spouse to offer you a different perspective.

Mediation is the path of least resistance in which you and your partner can sit with a neutral negotiator to develop a constructive, and mutually agreeable resolution for your "divide." With a mediator, an agreement can be made, divorce papers drawn and processed for under one hundred dollars.

A resource for mediators in Canada is Family Mediation (www.fmc.ca); resources within the United States include: The Association For Conflict Resolution (www.acrnet.org), and the Academy of Family Mediators (www.mediate.com). Other out-of-the-courthouse combinations include collaborative law and arbitration.

If no resolution is met through the mediation process, the next door to open is to the legal office. You find a divorce attorney in this legal game and roll the dice again. The following are several recommendations:

1. If you have the wish to marry again, generate a prenuptial agreement and miss the next three steps. Love is binding, but do not allow it to be blinding. This is a business deal laced with emotion, so let it be thought out, signed and agreed to while you are still sleeping in the same bed. Alison Sawyer's book *If You Love Me, Put It in Writing* is designed to help you write your own prenuptial agreement.

2. Seek legal counsel early. Understanding your legal rights and the laws brings clarity. Find a lawyer that is respected in the community; not all have the same qualifications and mastery in family law. The goal in finding a lawyer shall be to secure the best possible legal advice, not to find someone that agrees with you. Shark teeth, computer brain, spine of steel, heart of gold and dash of humour are found to be useful traits in a lawyer. (Thank you, my friend and legal counsel, Lynn Reierson, for being all this and more.)

3. Document everything. You are paying this lawyer to manage your case so listen to their advice and allow all correspondence to filter though their legal screen. Watch the contents of e-mails and off-the-emotional-cuff comments, for they will come back to bite you in the bum.

4. Use your lawyer as a resource for family psychologists, court parenting, as well as mediation courses and literature. With a pending divorce, you are almost a part of the majority; meaning, many others have done this before you. Listen to all the advice and take what feels most natural for your situation. Remembering your soon-to-be former spouse is also the person you fell in love with and married, and may also be the mother or father to your children – with whom you will share a lifetime. This divorce is not an isolated event, it is a lifetime process. If there are children involved, see the process through their eyes to keep a broad perspective.

The first legal match is a settlement conference. The lawyers from both sides meet, present and share information. They set their intention and a date with their clients and a judge. During this *intimate* gathering in the courtroom, the judge gives a recommendation based on the information presented within a few hours and it may be accepted or rejected by either or both parties. This judge's decision is likely a foreshadow of what might happen in a full trial, mostly to encourage couples to settle early with an agreement they both can endure. With cooperation from both sides, this can usually be arranged within a year of the divorce petition. Costs up to this point may be between $10,000 and $15,000.

Once again, there is an opportunity to settle with the judges' decision, or roll the dice again and proceed to the court of courts: a full trial. A full trial courtroom battle is what stirs the seas of stress for divorcing couples – as they give-up their control, their fate then lies in the hands and judgments of the court. The full trial process may extend over the course of nearly four to five months, and amount to an additional approximate-cost of $20,000. This is the part of the *game* that determines the *winner.* I use the word *winner* with tongue-stuck-in-cheek, as there are only players, but essentially no real winners of this game. The universe levels the playing field so each party has some sort of compromise.

The judge examines the admissible evidence (marital infidelity and financial circumstance are irrelevant in family law), and according to his opinion (based on probable truths) lays legal judgment for the providence of your children and dissolution of your marriage. As the referee, the judge makes a decision within a few hours that will effectively influence your family's life forever.

Once again, the laws of universal balance take-over, saying, *"If you cannot govern yourself, then you must be governed."* There are no winners or losers, just individuals testing the rules of the (universal) *game*. With wisdom and experience, Justice Harvey Brownstone beautifully writes a legal and compassionate understanding of the process in his book, entitled *Tug of War*.

In summary, the actual road to resolution of a divorce has many paths and variables. Meeting with your partner to decide your own terms of separation and having a divorce lawyer *stamp* the document is the most cost and time efficient way to settle a divorce. On the other hand, a full-blown trial with divorce lawyers and judges is the path that costs the most money, but also provides the wisdom in experiencing all the flavors. My intention is not to persuade you in any particular direction, but instead honoring your uniqueness by delivering a menu from which you may order your own plate of learning. I write with respect towards your personalized set of circumstances and with honor to the authenticity of your own path.

4

Swim In Stress

In 1929, Walter Cannon developed the theory of an *acute response* to a stimuli stating that animals react to threats with a change in their physiology and a general surge of the sympathetic nervous system to prepare for *fighting* or *fleeing*. Later, the actual word *stress* was termed by psychologist and endocrinologist, Hans Selye, to further describe the set of responses to stress, which he called General Adaptation Syndrome (GAS). Selye documented a secondary level of a stress response with his discovery of the development of a pathological state from on-going, unrelieved stress, or the inability of an organism to adapt to a stressful environment.

The sympathetic nervous system response to stress is an innate (inborn) physiological activation providing for the body's needs. The response stimulates dilation of the pupils in the eyes for more acute vision, vaso-dilation of arteries and veins to increase blood circulation, release of adrenaline for energy, and so forth. Stress may be physical or mental, real or imagined, and may be perceived by a multi-cellular human, or a simple-cell organism. In humans, stress includes an initial state of alarm - the adrenaline rush of *'fight or flight,'* short or long-term coping strategies or resistance, and end-stage exhaustion. The sympathetic symptoms may also include: increased heart rate, increased blood pressure, increased gastric acids in the stomach, sweating, irritability, sleep disturbances and heartburn.

Through the process of a divorce emotions may be running wild: living arrangements changing, dividing of assets, custody battles, separation of parent from child perhaps. Not to mention, relaying updates and talking through all of this with legal counsel, family, and friends – if a divorcee is *not* having a *stress reaction* during this experience, please check for a pulse! This stress reaction is the surest sign of being *alive*! It is a normal, and natural physiological response to stressful stimuli. This is intentionally how the body works. The body's natural defense mechanism designed to keep humans and animals alive is always present in different forms and continually assists the body in adapting to a changing environment.

Stress is a fact of life, always present in different forms. Yesterday it may have been a family illness; last year maybe the death of a loved one, and today it is your divorce. Congratulations, you are now another divorce statistic, and – as mentioned previously – a part of the majority. I respectfully acknowledge your innate response and offer the tools and ideas for empowering balance back into your life.

Moving and molding within the challenge defines the character and circumstance. As a martial artist, I learned blocking a punch really hurts. But to allow it – mindfully diverting the blow in another direction – diffuses the attacking energy. It is not as painful, uses less energy, and the *attacker* becomes weary. Acknowledge the situation, and then attempt to diffuse the situation with honor and respect. Sometimes, however, if a bully continues attacking, it may require a (figurative or literal) punch in the nose to stop them in order to maintain one's own dignity and domain. This is similar to a divorce match. The success of a *victor* comes not through what happens, but how one responds to it. Remember at the end of a sparing match to always bow to your opponent in honor of the opportunity.

In any event, an adrenaline sympathetic nervous system stress response must be modulated with physical exercise or movement. Evolution has designed the animal-like defense response in a way to increase blood circulation to provide animals the power and blood supply to meet the need for fighting or escaping a predator. The best way to metabolize the stress hormones the brain releases is to expel energy and sweat, with a heart rate-raising exercise routine. Cognitive and emotional benefits of exercise seem to be a result of an increase in nerve cell growth (neurogenesis) in an area in the brain called the hippocampus. Aerobics, quick-burst training, power-walking, biking, running, swimming, weight lifting, climactic orgasm – any activity resulting in sweating – will metabolize molecules of emotional stress to reset a brain balance. My salvation was to arm myself with my *iPod* of loud rock music, clip it onto my belt, put on my running shoes, and sing to the top of my lungs, running-off my divorce.

The following disciplines, techniques, and activities are other fundamental practices for not only thriving through stress of divorce, but also for vitality in life – to tune into the universal principles and unify mind, body and spirit.

Meditation – A calming technique to balance one's perspective is meditation, employing controlled breathing and centered focus. "Performance Breath" (*Appendix A*), included at the end of this book, is an article representing the importance of the breath, as well as a few other meditative exercises. Yoga is a therapeutic modality beautifully combining basic meditative principles into artful movements and positioning.

Eating well and supplementation – In times of transitional stress, proper nutritional intake is most important for optimizing mental and physical function. As stress increases, the metabolism of vitamins and minerals also increases – B-vitamins in particular. Eating cruciferous vegetables, fruits, and proteins supplies the body with necessary fuel. Avoiding refined sugars, dairy and other processed foods, alcohol, and caffeine helps to reduce the metabolic stress load by decreasing (internal) inflammatory processes. The latter four substances create a micro-stress environment with reactions and symptoms similar to the 'fight-or-flight' response you are trying to dissolve. Essential fatty acids (namely, Omega-3 fatty-acids ALA, DHA, and EPA), complex multi-vitamins, as well as mineral supplementation are the bare essentials. If you are interested in more details for your specific needs, *Adeeva* nutritionals (www.adeeva.com) offers complimentary individualized lifestyle and nutritional assessments.

Sunlight exposure and fresh air – All living organisms absorb energy from the sun and the earth, so move out of the indoor concrete cage and spend time outside, in nature, gardening, hiking, and playing.

Listen to the music – With respect to my previous comment of singing at the top of my lungs, there are many healing effects that come through listening to music. Musical notes vibrate at different frequencies. These frequencies resonate within our structure and mobilize energy. There are some authors such as Andrews, Cousto and Goldman that pair certain notes to the different energy centers in the body. Music helps people connect with the vibration of the universe. The details of this statement may be found in Kelper's *Music of the Spheres*, Hindu philosophies, and within music history theories. Whether a yogi chanting OM at 136 Hz, or a Christian singing *Amen*, the importance of music in attaching balance of the spirit to the mind and body is a universal truth.

Therapeutic journaling - After brushing-over the topics of health concerning the body swimming through stress, let's delve into the recesses of the mind and learn how to float thoughts. Our words are the bridge between our mind and our actions. So, writing-out thoughts can be therapeutic. I would often start my *therapeutic* journaling page with: *"That F****** B******! How could he do this? What an As*****."* Venting, and releasing strong emotions is indeed therapeutic, to an extent. However, the skillful practice with journaling is to transition thoughts and writing into the energy you wish to carry on with you, always ending the journaling in gratitude with *thank you*.

Admittedly, my degree in psychology didn't prepare me for this therapy, but my instincts say if the thought is within your mind, bring it out for examination. The thoughts in your mind that remain unexpressed become repressed in the body and manifest as *dis*-ease. Write-out your feelings, asking yourself why they exist. What is the real issue that is being challenged? No one or nothing can make you feel anything without your consent. In fact, I believe others are brought to us to reflect our own insecurities so that we may learn. The perceived obstacles are undeniably opportunities in disguise. Capture them; capitalize on their presence. Regardless of the nasty words written on the pages before me, I continued to write and examined my emotions until I could say, "Thank you God for showing me this, for now I may learn about myself and others." Arriving to an understanding that everything is perfect just as it is.

I admit, occasionally it took me *weeks* to finish just one page, and even now there is always new material. Concentrating on who is right or wrong creates a subjective veil of emotion; while basking in the glory of what *is*, carries your life's spark. Be honest with yourself, try to see the other perspective and at the end of this chapter write your own thank you note.

Also included at the end of this book is a guide for creating affirmations, "Affirmations To Abundance" (*Appendix B*). The purpose of an affirmation is to commit a passive idea into an active intention to ensure the conscious learning moment. The tangible thought guides the actions that dictate your destiny.

Joseph Campbell once said, "The schizophrenic is drowning in the same waters in which the mystic is swimming with delight." Take the ideas in this chapter, choose your course and swim through the seas of stress.

Divinity in Divorce: Tranquility In Gratitude & Love

5

The Kids Will Be Okay

One of the first questions most parents consider in divorce is, "How will this affect the children?" In fact, without quoting a particular statistic, it may be one of the most important predictors of why parents stay married. I was married for ten years with two boys – five and eight years old at the time of separation – and I would do anything to protect them. Usually, the nurturer (or gatherer) performs household activities, while a provider (or hunter) works *outside the hut* to bring home the *bacon*. In our case, the thought of having to disrupt our boys' lives by creating chaos in a "broken" family, with a shared custody arrangement, kept us married for years. My parents separated after their forty years of marriage just two years before I did. The eventual perception of my parent's family unit expanding instead of dissolving made it permissible for me to do the same to transform my marriage.

Divorce may seem like a single event, but parenting is a process that unfolds over a lifetime. Children are in the heart of parents to ensure our focus on the lifelong learning of love, not without all of its dynamic components. It is through a connection with our children that parents are granted love and wisdom.

S.O.S. distress call line for divorce sends the following bits of practical advice for taking care of the children through a divorce:

1. **Manage your own feelings first.** Helping yourself helps your children. As the recommendation in an airplane pre-flight safety video: *if you are traveling with children, place the oxygen mask first on yourself before assisting them.* Seek the help of family, friends, and therapists of mind, body and spirit to bring yourself into balance. Read, pray, and ask for guidance to help you see this as just an event to strengthen and bring you all closer to love.

2. **Build a support network.** For immediate help visit the Emergency department of your local hospital, or call 911. Seek shelters for abused women/men, call distress support-lines if necessary. A family lawyer may assist with building a support network for emotional support, and may provide recommendations for a family psychologist, an accountant, an estate planner, or other specialized professionals to assist with practical details. Family, friends, counsellors, teachers, neighbours, coaches, family law divisions, libraries, and

community support centers are other resources. Ask for what you need, have faith that help is available, and receive it with gratitude when it arrives.

3. **Assure your children of your love.** As a heart link, the children often become tools for parents to manipulate one another. Children may think a divorce is their fault and that their parents will get back-together if they keep them happy – so they too are participants. They worry about having to take sides and trying to please both parents. My children will complain to me about their father as they will complain to him about me. Be confident in your decision, respect the other parent in front of the children and avoid putting them in the middle of your spousal electricity. I watched a family court teaching-video that was a humbling experience; I heard *my* words repeated on the tape, putting my children in the middle to relay messages to my spouse. *"Tell your father to pick you up at noon;"* or worse, *"Your father always keeps the new clothes at his house."* I wish everyone could watch this video and partake in a family court course; for it was an instrumental tool for gaining perspective. Spend time alone with each of your children every day and ask how they are doing. Listen, and acknowledge their feelings. Confirm and reconfirm your love with your words and actions. In matters of the heart there is only one truth – right or wrong depends on your perspective.

4. **Children need both parents.** Unique issues may arise if there is family violence, drug abuse or mental illness that require special consideration. But even in these circumstances, research shows that children do best when both parents are involved in the child's life – if merely with supervised visits. Parenting styles will be different because, as I have mentioned before, in a spouse we attract the opposite. Is it not the variety of parenting tactics that create adaptability? According to Darwin's theories, essential adaptability supports survival, growth and evolution. Species that are tested and challenged in different environments become stronger with greater chance of survival. Seeing the dualities in our existence, and understanding the universal laws of balance helps us predict and find comforting security within our environment. If there is a *health nut* parent on one end of the divorce, there will be a *junk-food* parent on the other. One parent may encourage technology and the other may not. One parent may be more concerned about the outer appearance and one more about the inner experience. If one is an over-protector, then the other is an over-aggressor. It is just both sides of a parental coin in the dualities of humanity.

5. **Practice humble confidence with honesty.** As there are hidden agendas to expose the other parent, there are also tendencies to hide some of their forbidden parts. The children do not need all the details of the marriage and divorce, but they do

need you to clearly state *your* position and feelings. For example, "Your father and I have different ideas and opinions about *this* and it is challenging for us to see each other's point of view." This is an honest statement communicating the truth to the children, validating emotions without blame or shame, and without pressure placed upon them to choose a side. It is not always possible to follow the ideals of presenting a unified parental presence for the children (in marriage or divorce). The best we can do is to accept emotions as stepping stones towards growth. Identify your own emotions – admitting they are based upon your own values and perception justifies the emotions. Having emotions is okay; allow your spouse and children to have and own their emotions as well. This nurturing and processing grooms their emotional intelligence for life. If you are too emotional to deal with a certain issue, then request the support of a guidance counsellor, family psychologist, teacher or family friend that will help your children find a balanced perspective. It is not what happens to you, but what you do with it that determines the outcome. Instilling inspiration – not manipulation – is a more distinguished and dignified approach. Ghandi says, "We must be the change we wish to see in the world."

As I continue to meet with *perceived* obstacles along my journey, I ask myself how do they serve my children? Do they create more independence? In a particular situation, do my children have to learn to ask specifically for what they love? Is this process developmental? Will these challenges teach them to draw upon resources to make them stronger? It is an empowering experience to remove judgment and observe the situation through all the eyes viewing the picture.

Let me illustrate an exercise I practiced with my (our) boys on one of the many nights they wished their father and I were still together.

I said, "Boys, I understand your wishes to have things return to the way they were with all of us living together. Instead of longing, let's explore a game of love. Instead of just focusing on what you think you have lost, let's focus on the areas where you have gained." So then I asked, "What do you now have at your Papa's house that you never had here? What are the three things that you love there, at his house?"

The first answer was, "Cats!" With my family's allergies we did not ever have furry pets.

"Great. What else?"

"Papa gives us *Gatorade* for our lunch." Not my choice in drink, I had to bite my tongue and remind myself this exercise was not about me, it was for the boys.

"Good; and this makes you happy, yes? And you don't have this at my house. Okay, what else do you like about Papa's that you did not have when we were living together?"

"Papa lets us play a video game that you would not allow." Once again, seeing the world through their eyes. My first thought was to get on the phone and blast my *FS* (former spouse) for allowing them to play this computer war-game; yet again, this was not about me. If I lose the children's perspectives I cannot be present with them.

I responded, "Wow, it sounds like you really have fun with Papa in ways that you didn't when we were together." I am not changing my rules or values, instead I am respecting that his are different than mine. When I felt that my values were being tested, a phrase I often repeated to myself was "What doesn't kill them will make them stronger."

I said to the boys, "Now, let's look at what you have *here* at my place that you love. What is first?"

"The garden hose," was their reply. Not exactly the *love and hugs* answer I was expecting, but remembered it was not about me, it was about honoring the children.

"Good. And yes, in the summer you guys have lots of fun in the sprinkler and spraying each other with the hose."

Another response was, "The swing set in the backyard." And finally, that I helped them find things they had lost.

This conversation gave me a great deal of insight into what is really important to them; how they feel is expressed through their responses of a garden-hose verses *Gatorade*. Just being present and listening allots them the opportunity to explore their own feelings in a safe, non-judgmental environment. To understand their values and be able to listen to their voice (over my own) was an exercise in love.

Somehow it became important for me to say I was following my own heart in making the decision to divorce. I did not do it just for them (in a selfless sacrifice), or just for me (in a selfish action), but truly a combination of the two. I trusted that this challenge would make us all stronger, more self-reliant, independent, and more on-purpose as a family; that through the emotions of anger, shock and grief we would all eventually find a balance of love. I maintain a faith in my choice and a faith that some day they will come to respect and understand our decision.

6

Laugh It Out

Laughing stimulates the integration of the mind, body and spirit. Laughing mends a broken heart, improves the immune system, decreases stress, relaxes muscles and the nervous system, allows deep emotions to rise to the surface, shifts perspectives, releases inhibitions and helps to identify judgment – as others are drawn to you to share the same.

This closing chapter highlights fun quotes and stories to encourage laughter. Amongst your laughter, you may find yourself and your spouse within these stories, as the truest of truths are found through humor.

We all have a set of values that we follow. For some, spending time with the family is most important and seen as a way to love; while for others, loving is building a home or a strong financial foundation. Some feel sexual intercourse is the way to express love, and others express love by offering gifts, compliments, time or money. In marriage *and* divorce your spouse is there to test your values, as they will likely have an opposite set to your own.

Dr. John Demartini's more realistic view is, "The whole purpose of love is to find someone that has a balance of values that support and challenge your own and marry them." Knowing what is important to your partner, loving them as they wish to be loved – yet at the same time respecting and honoring your own values – is the creative process of true love and grace. Judgment and labels arise when you expect another to fit into *your* value system (rather than honoring their own). We shall all do our best with what we have, know and believe.

Divorce Quotes

"I've never been married, but I tell people I'm divorced so they won't think something's wrong with me."
~ *Elayne Boosler*

"It wasn't until I got divorced that I understood the value of money." ~ *Melanie B*

"Many divorces are not really the result of irreparable injury, but involve, instead, a desire on the part of the man or woman to shatter the set-up, start-out from scratch alone, and make life work for them all over again. They want the risk of disaster, want to touch bottom, see where bottom is, and, coming up, to breathe the air with relief and relish again." ~ *Edward Hoagland*

"When two people decide to get a divorce, it isn't a sign that they *don't* understand one another, but a sign that they have, at last, begun to." ~ *Helen Rowland*

"I guess the only way to stop divorce is to stop marriage."
~ *Will Rogers*

"I'm an excellent housekeeper. Every time I get a divorce, I keep the house." ~ *Zsa Zsa Gabor*

"I'd marry again if I found a man who had fifteen million and would sign over half of it to me before the marriage and guarantee he'd be dead within a year." ~ *Bette Davis*

"I don't think I'll get married again. I'll just find a woman I don't like and give her a house." ~ *Lewis Grizzard*

"I have often wanted to drown my troubles, but I can't get my wife to go swimming." ~ *Jimmy Carter*

"My advice to you is get married: if you find a good wife you'll be happy; if not, you'll become a philosopher."
~ *Socrates*

"I believe in the institution of marriage, and I intend to keep trying till I get it right." ~ *Richard Pryor*

"A great marriage is not when the "perfect couple" comes together. It is when an imperfect couple learns to enjoy their differences." ~ *Dave Meurer*

"Ah, yes, divorce, from the Latin word meaning to rip out a man's genitals through his wallet." ~ *Robin Williams*

Divinity in Divorce: Tranquility In Gratitude & Love

"That's When The Fight Started" – source know as *Judy*

My wife and I were watching *Who Wants To Be A Millionaire Quiz* on television while we were in bed.

I turned to her and said, "Do you want to make love?"

"No," she answered.

I then said, "Is that your final answer?" She didn't even look at me this time, simply implying *yes*. So I said, "Then I'd like to phone a friend."

And that's when the fight started.

I asked my wife, "Where do you want to go for our anniversary?" It warmed my heart to see her face melt in sweet appreciation.

"Somewhere I haven't been in a long time!" She said.

So I suggested, "How about the kitchen?"

And that's when the fight started.

Saturday morning I got up early, quietly dressed, made my lunch, grabbed the dog, and slipped quietly into the garage. I hooked up the boat to the truck, and proceeded to back out into a torrential downpour. The wind was blowing 50 mph, so I pulled back into the garage, turned on the radio, and discovered that the weather would be bad all day.

I went back into the house, quietly undressed, and slipped back into bed. I cuddled up to my wife's back, now with a different anticipation, and whispered, "The weather out there is terrible."

My loving wife of ten years replied, "Can you believe my stupid husband is out fishing in that?"

And that's when the fight started.

A man and a woman were asleep like two innocent babies. Suddenly, at three o'clock in the morning, a loud noise came from outside.

The woman, bewildered, jumped up from the bed and yelled at the man, "*Holy crap*! That must be my husband!"

So the man hopped out of the bed, scared and naked jumped out the window. He smashed himself on the ground, ran through a thorn bush and to his car as fast as he could go.

A few minutes later he returned and went up to the bedroom and screamed at the woman, "I *am* your husband!"

The woman yelled back, "Yeah, then why were you running?"

And that's when the fight started.

I tried to talk my wife into buying a case of *Miller Light* for $14.95. Instead, she bought a jar of cold cream for $7.95. I told her the beer would make her look better at night than the cold cream.

And that's when the fight started.

A woman was standing nude, looking in the bedroom mirror. She was not happy with what she saw and said to her husband, "I feel horrible; I look old, fat and ugly. I really need you to pay me a compliment."

The husband replies, "Your eye-sight is damn near perfect."

And that's when the fight started.

Closing with quotes and funny stories, sharing other perceptions and values is so you may learn to embrace all parts of you and your former spouse in this process. This integration allows your spirit to soar in light of finding *Divinity In Divorce*.

Appendix A
Performance Breath

"With just breath, soul, and courage, the man achieved a life to be admired." ~ *Upanishads*

Breathing is the essence of life. Athletes and yogis are masters at working with the breath. But many adults have forgotten the powerful natural of breathing we all clearly understood at birth. A few insights:

Breath Is Energy

The scientific definition of breathing and cell respiration:

> Inhalation is the transport of oxygen to the cells where it reacts with glucose to give water, carbon dioxide and an energy molecule called adenosine triphosphate (ATP). The exhalation releases carbon dioxide, nitric oxide, and water (amongst other waste molecules), while ATP energy may be stored.

Breathe Optimizes Performance

For athletes, a lot of training relates to breathing. During an endurance event, efficient ATP (energy) supply derived from oxygen intake is necessary to maximize strength and endurance. The inhaled oxygen enhances performance while exhaling carbon dioxide and nitric oxide improve flexibility and recovery times.

Breath Is Healing

Medical and behavioral physiologists report the negative effects of retaining too much carbon dioxide. Many different illnesses may be associated with inefficient breathing that has a negative effect on acid-base (pH) physiology, electrolyte balance of sodium and potassium, hemoglobin affinity in oxygen distribution, kidney function markers of bicarbonates and sodium, and EEG brain wave patterns. Acid reflux, anxiety, depression, weight gain, cardiovascular and kidney disease are a few conditions that may improve with more efficient breathing.

Breath Is Divine

The yoga literature on breath unites these scientific truths from the microcosmic cell to the macrocosmic universe. When we breathe we share the same atoms from the cell membrane, out into the air, into the atmosphere and beyond. Metaphysically, this sharing of energy electrons connects each of us to a greater cosmic commodity.

Breathing consciously generates vital ATP energy. Through inhalation you experience your full potential. Exhalation is a sacred act of surrendering or releasing all you are to the universe, smelly gases included. Through calming mental chatter, lowering blood pressure and heart rate, releasing lactic acid from tissues – increasing metabolism – physiology can be regulated through breathing!

Take time for a "Performance Breath"

1. Lie on your back or sit in a comfortable position with your natural spinal curves maintained or supported, with hands palms-up on the floor beside you or on your lap.

2. Inhale slowly through your nose for a full four to five seconds. Stay aware of the feeling of your breath as it passes through your nostrils, slowly expands your rib cage filling your lungs, and finally pushes into your abdomen so you can see and feel your belly rise with air. Then, hold the full inhale for several seconds.

3. Gently release your breath, slowly bringing awareness and focus to following it with your mind in the reverse order – from belly depressing to lungs relaxing. Notice the quality and quantity of air as you exhale. Then hold the exhale for a few seconds until at the very end when your body again calls for air. The pause at the top of the inhale and the bottom of the exhale creates a quieting of the mind into a present meditative moment.

4. With your eyes closed, gently imagine every cell relaxing, being massaged by the breath as it sweeps past.

5. Repeat this *three* times for energy, *five* times for relaxation, and *eight* times for great lovemaking!

Appendix B

Affirmations To Abundance

Our words are the connection between our imagined thoughts and our actions of reality. They reflect our thoughts, allow us to communicate with our environment and seed the earth to grow towards our destiny. Thus, transforming our language is the most efficient blueprint to creating our dreams and desires.

The written words of ancient texts, great leaders, authors and poets are celebrated for the impact on individuals and nations. Words that relay knowledge, spark inspiration, and stimulate novel thoughts survive centuries. An idea represented in a sentence – with a subject, a verb and a noun – sets the stage for designing the direction of an idea, and describes the action it may accomplish. When strung together in this way an *affirmation* is birthed. An affirmation is the assertion that the idea or thought exists. As it exits, then it is real.

The Internet has millions of articles tagged for affirmations; the multitude of *law of attraction* writers – and others in the self-help genre – have books and manuals of affirmations to assist with manifesting greatness. Programming and reprogramming the words and sentences you use brings shape to the shapeless, hope to the hopeless, power to the powerless, and further perpetuates the boundless sea of possibility.

Below are examples of Affirmations:

> "I love and approve of myself. I am at peace. I am calm. All is well." ~ Louise Hay

> "I have a dream that one day this nation will rise up and live out the true meaning of its creed: We hold these truths to be self-evident, that all men are created equal." ~ Martin Luther King, Jr.

> "Let us therefore brace ourselves to our duties, and so bear ourselves that, if the British Empire and its Commonwealth last for a thousand years, men will still say, *this was their finest hour*." ~ Sir Winston Churchill

Whether for an individual, a Country or an Empire these affirmations have a subject and an intention that has the power to change beliefs and thoughts and create realities. There are a few guidelines that are consistent in the most powerful affirmations:

1. Let an affirmation be in the present tense, as if it is happening *now*. This is the moment that erases the past and designs a destiny for the future.

2. Use words and thoughts that you love without including words you do not love. "I have divine health" verses "I do not want to be sick."

3. Short, clear and detailed affirmations make it easier to encode, focus and manifest exactly what you love.

The world is an abundance of endless possibilities; choose all that you love and dream *BIG*! Many people are so caught up in their current situation or perceived problem they lose the ability to envision a solution. Dream up scenarios, take the best ideas, write them down and act on them.

"All men dream but not equally. Those who dream by night in the dusky recesses of their minds wake in the day to find that it was vanity; but the dreamers of the day are dangerous men, for they may act their dream with open eyes to make it possible."
~ T.E. Lawrence

References

1. Andrews, Ted. *Sacred Sounds - Magic And Healing Through Words And Music.* Woodbury, Minnesota: Llewellyn Publications, 1992.
2. Braden, Gregg. *The Divine Matrix - Bridging Time, Space Miracles And Belief.* Carlsbad, California, New York, London, Sydney, Johannesburg, Vancouver, Hong Kong, New Delhi: Hay House, Inc, 2007.
3. Brownstone, Harvey Justice. *Tug of War.* Ontario: ECW Press, 2009.
4. Cousto, Hans. *The Cosmic Octave - Origin of Harmony.* Mendocino, California: Life Rhythm Publication, 2000.
5. Demartini, John F. *The Breakthrough Experience: A Revolutionary New Approach to Personal Transformation.* Carlsbad, California, London, Sydney, Johannesburg, Vancouver, Hong Kong, Mumbai: Hay House, Inc. 2002.
6. Descartes, Rene. *Descartes Selected Philosophical Writings.* New York: Cambridge University Press, 1988.
7. Gibran, Kahlil. *The Prophet.* New York: Alfred A. Knope, Inc, 1923.
8. Goldman, Jonathan. *Shifting Frequencies.* Flagstaff, AZ: Light Technology Publishing, 1998.
9. Gottman, John. *Raising An Emotionally Intelligent Child.* New York: Simon & Schuster, 1997.
10. Leibniz, G.W. *Discourse On Metaphysics And Other Essays.* New York: Prometheus Books, 1992.
11. Sawyer, Alison. *If You Love Me Put It In Writing.* Self Counsel Press, 2008.
12. Talbot, Michael. *The Holographic Universe.* New York: Harper Collins Publishers, 1991.
13. Pert, Candace. B, PhD. *Molecules Of Emotion.* New York: Simon & Schuster Inc., 1999.
14. Public Health Canada. *Helping Children and Youth Live with Separation and Divorce.* Ontario: Publications Public Health Agency of Canada, 2001.
15. Wolf, Anthony PhD. *Why Did You Have To Get A Divorce? And When Can I Get A Hamster: A Guide To Parenting Through Divorce.* New York: The Noonday Press, 1998.

Divinity in Divorce: Tranquility In Gratitude & Love

About Dr. Dena G. Churchill

Dr. Dena Churchill, chiropractor and dynamic keynote speaker, is especially admired for her ability to deeply connect to audiences around the world with clarity, wit, wisdom and compassion. With a humble confidence, she draws from a wealth of real-life experiences to guide people towards their visions and achieving their best. Through writing and speaking, she illustrates ideas informative as well as entertaining, offering ageless wisdom of the trillium of mind, body, spirit balance in healing and transformation.

As a doctor of chiropractic, professional speaker and consultant, Dr. Churchill integrates her extensive studies in psychology, biology, chiropractic, acupuncture, and energy healing to provide audiences with fresh concepts in healing and transformation.

As a successful chiropractor based in Halifax, Nova Scotia, she adjusts the spine to optimize nervous system function and enhance whole-being wellness. Through her company, *Trillium Transformational Seminars*, she offers informative, engaging, and often humorous seminars to present practical ideas to captivate, motivate and inspire audiences to learn techniques for living with greater purpose and clarity. She practices to liberate the mind and dissolve emotional stress that interferes with healing processes.

Dr. Churchill loves travelling, having studied internationally in Greece, Turkey, Cuba, South Africa, Australia, the United States, and the United Kingdom. Outside the borders of Beijing, China, she worked and studied at one of the world's most prestigious traditional Chinese Medicine hospitals.

To keep a balance in her life as she moves between patients, parents, audiences and children, Dena is still running and doing yoga. Dr. Dena is whom she is because of the family around her that makes all things possible. Her sons Dominic and Gabriel, Mother Betty Lou (office manager), Sister Jody (accountant) and Father Howard (Children's Taxi) offer daily wisdom of love and reflection.

With her special interest in children's health and education, she is networking with the Complimentary Medicine Departments of the local Children's Hospital and Dalhousie Medical School. Dr. Dena Churchill is a wellness expert featured on CBS's television show *Health Matters*; she also writes as a contributing author to *Health and Wellness Magazine, OptiMYz.*

To secure speaking events, or for seminar and program registration, she invites you to visit her online at the following web address: www.drdenachurchill.com.

What Others Are Saying

"Dr. Dena Churchill is brilliant, articulate and inspiring. She has the ability to make you think, laugh and even bring you to tears with her fountain of inspiration." ~ Dr. John F. Demartini, chiropractor, speaker, and bestselling author of *The Breakthrough Experience – A Revolutionary New Approach to Personal Transformation*

"Dr. Churchill pulls off a top-notch show; we all marveled at her presence and stunning beauty. After listening to her speak, a member of our audience said, *"Now she should be on Oprah."* ~ Jenny Kierstead, writer in the *Daily News* and founder of *Breathing Space Yoga Studios* in Halifax and Bedford, NS

"Extremely interesting, solid knowledge base, offered me new perspective." ~ Jeannette E. Combes, President Occupational Health Nurses Association of Nova Scotia

"Dr. Dena Churchill exudes passion, clarity, and certainty that invites listeners to invest with trust in her message of hope and possibility. The world needs to hear what she has to say, in both speech and through writing." ~ Peter Davison, 2008 President, Halifax Chapter, Canadian Association of Professional Speakers

INTERNATIONAL HEALTH PUBLISHING

Inspiring and challenging the world to experience the light, International Health Publishing's mission is to create publications expressing the truth, encouraging spiritual enlightenment, facilitating growth and healing – while also providing a phenomenal reading experience.

INTERNATIONAL HEALTH PUBLISHING

Little and Growing

(978) 846-1964

www.InternationalHealthPublishing.com

www.ingramcontent.com/pod-product-compliance
Lightning Source LLC
Chambersburg PA
CBHW020021050426
42450CB00005B/580